PECULIAR PETS

2021

Awesome Animals

Edited By Donna Samworth

First published in Great Britain in 2021 by:

Young Writers
Remus House
Coltsfoot Drive
Peterborough
PE2 9BF
Telephone: 01733 890066
Website: www.youngwriters.co.uk

Printed and bound in the UK by BookPrintingUK
Website: www.bookprintinguk.com
YB0476L

★ FOREWORD ★

Welcome Reader!

Are you ready to discover weird and wonderful creatures that you'd never even dreamed of?

For Young Writers' latest competition we asked primary school pupils to create a Peculiar Pet of their own invention, and then write a poem about it! They rose to the challenge magnificently and the result is this fantastic collection full of creepy critters and amazing animals!

Here at Young Writers our aim is to encourage creativity in children and to inspire a love of the written word, so it's great to get such an amazing response, with some absolutely fantastic poems. Not only have these young authors created imaginative and inventive animals, they've also crafted wonderful poems to showcase their creations and their writing ability. These poems are brimming with inspiration. The slimiest slitherers, the creepiest crawlers and furriest friends are all brought to life in these pages – you can decide for yourself which ones you'd like as a pet!

I'd like to congratulate all the young authors in this anthology, I hope this inspires them to continue with their creative writing.

★ CONTENTS ★

Spencer Mitchell (10)	66
Max Tighe (10)	69
Lucie-Rose Stubbs (9)	70
Evelynn Trewhitt (9)	73
Heidi Singh (11)	74
Oscar Lund (11)	76
Charlie Cupples (11)	78
Jack Molyneux (11)	80
Lucy Peirse-Pallister (9)	82
Mollie Scott (8)	85
Echo Trewhitt (10)	86
Elizabeth Swinhoe (10)	88
Joshua Mitcheson (9)	91
Noah Rushforth (10)	92
Finley Dee (9)	95
Lola Sill (10)	96
Charlie Briggs (9)	99
Leonie Mitchell (10)	100
Elliott Worton (9)	103
Summer Markland (10)	104
Reiley Clark-Wood (9)	107
Archie Turner (10)	108
Sienna Jones (9)	111
Chloe Jones (11)	112
Leon Morris-Hall (11)	114
Erin-Rose Cawley (9)	116
Tiana Floyd (9)	119
Josie Kretowicz (9)	120
Layla Earl (9)	123
Coby Waller	124
Imogen Banbridge (8)	127
Reece Clark-Wood (10)	128
Alfie Rayson (9)	130
Adam Robinson (9)	133
Heidi Swales (11)	134
Harvey Nawton-Tunnicliffe (10)	136
Luca Charlton (11)	138
Steven Porteous (11)	140
Spencer Worton (11)	142
Onyx Clarke (11)	144
Kayden Hoyle (10)	146
Alice Kent (9)	148
Tulisa Willis (9)	150

Harvey Fryett (9)	151

Orchard Primary School, Lambeth

Hodan Musa (9)	152
Rafsan Ramin (9)	153
Abdullah Malik (9)	154
Abdullah Yahga Umari (8)	155
Mikaeel Haruna (9)	156
Bilal Ahmed (9)	157
Masud Abdi (9)	158
Mubarakat Ajetunmobi (8)	159
Abdullahi Hassan (9)	160
Ayaan Hussain (9)	161
Adam Gacem (9)	162
Hanna Ahmed (9)	163
Hafsa Haji (9)	164
Abdulsemiu Rasheed (9)	165
Mohamed Hassan (8)	166
Mustafa Mohamed (8)	167

St Laurence CE Junior School, Ramsgate

Kali Groom (8)	168
Huie Thomas (8)	169
Taylor Bradley (8)	170
Harry Alger (8)	171
Emily Walendowska (8)	172
Darcie Bath (8)	173
Oliver Purton (8)	174
Elsie Rayner (8)	175
Connor Gillespie (7)	176
Mily Packman (8)	177
Ava Rich (8)	178
Laiton Smith (8)	179
Mylo Baker (7)	180
Isabelle Andrews (8)	181
Charlie Holt (8)	182
Tyler Hoare (7)	183
Sophie Harris (8)	184
Darcie Carnell (7)	185
Alfie Smithson (7)	186
Dylan Abram (8)	187

| Peter Taylor (8) | 188 |
| Ella Davies (8) | 189 |

Teesside High School, Eaglescliffe

Teddy Lane (11)	190
Hadi Younis (11)	192
Martha Shakesheff (11)	194
Ava Jeavons (10)	196
Louis Main (11)	197
Coco Hawkings (11)	198
Maisie Crowther (11)	199
Ellie Charlton (10)	200
Monty Shepherd (11)	201

THE
POEMS

COME ON SLO̲W COACH

My Vicious, Flying Robotic Octocat

Cold was the night at sea with wind blowing in my face
Lonely, there was an octopus, it seemed strange so I took it home
It had legs that looked like paws, it seemed like it was glitching from electricity
It was only me in the house
As soon as I finished homework I ran upstairs and jumped on my bed
As I was closing my eyes... *boom!*
The octopus removed his decoy outfit
Wings popped out, the octopus was robotic and had a cat face (a vicious cat face!)
I ran down and tied a knot to one of the legs so it wouldn't get loose
Turns out it had buttons, something pressed 'wild mode' so that explains everything
It was friendly, it ate my hair so I went bald
It became my pet after a while.

Lawrence Hurtado (10)
Allen Edwards Primary School, Stockwell

Terry The Teleporting Turtle

Terry the teleporting turtle is as peculiar as can be
With his emerald-green shell and his wonderful smile
He's definitely dazzling me
And the star on his belly, oh how wonderfully bright
In the morning, he's at my side
Then when I am ready, all ready for school
I climb atop his wonderful hexagon back
And in a whoosh and flashes of blue, white and green
We are at my school gate
So of course I am never late, oh Terry is a fabulous pet
But his day is not done oh far, far from that
A quick wave goodbye and whoosh, he's off
He's the kindest of folk so as soon as he pops off he's looking for someone to help
Then, hoorah, he's got a call on his favourite phone as green as the freshest of grass

So he is off to help that person
Then after the whoosh and the blue, white and green
Come considerable thanks
He can't stick around, he's not being mean
He's just got more people to help
On his next teleport though, he's greeted with something strange
On the ground, sitting there right in front of him
Is a little meek squirrel holding a tiny phone
The squirrel climbs on and although he doesn't normally teleport animals
He asks, "Where to?"
And the squirrel replies, "That tree over there, the one as tall as a tower block!"
Now Terry the teleporting turtle as peculiar as can be
Has a service where he teleports animals, people and me.

Joshua Agulnik (10)
Allen Edwards Primary School, Stockwell

Polly My Parrot

Polly my peculiar parrot
Has psychic powers
He is very stinky
As he hates showers

When he is helpful with his mind
I think he is being kind
But there are times when he is not
Which happens quite a lot!

The parrot annoys me, he does
He intently watches bees that buzz
Bwark! Bawark! he kind of sings
And then he does the most amazing thing...

With his mind
He bends the iron
Of the cage
Then he hops out onto a book, onto the left-hand
page

Then Polly my parrot takes flight
And then chases the bee that went out of the
window into the night

Then my parrot Polly
Stops right there, right still

Then he uses his second skill
While he stays there very still
He looks into the future
To see what is happening there

He discovers he wouldn't have caught the bee
That is what he sees
So, right still, right there where he stands
He shuts his eyes and goes to sleep!

Ben Agulnick (11)
Allen Edwards Primary School, Stockwell

Max The Chef

When I went to a gigantic tree
I saw a marvellous monkey
I took him home
Before I knew it he started to cook
He washed the plates
I took him to the vets and he started to bake
He had nothing wrong
I named him Max the chef
So he would be happy to be a chef
When he started to cook eggs
He did it quickly, even using his legs
Max took care of other animals, even cooked for them
Max is a genius, even smarter than a vet, he is smarter than him
Maz is as quiet as a mouse, he never speaks
Max is faster than a cheetah
He always wins races
Max is as gentle as a rabbit
Max is thick like a bear
Max is crazy for banana, he even plants it

He likes challenges and always enters them
That is my peculiar pet.

Elias Valdiviezo de Luis
Allen Edwards Primary School, Stockwell

Furry The Snake

Furry is the name of my pet
Furry is funny, yes she is
She is smarter than many other pets I have seen in
years!
Furry likes bows and make-up
But mess with her and you will never be able to
wake up!
Furry is tiny but also dangerous
One strike of her venom and you will sit still for
ages
Furry is sassy but not too much
And she has loads of friends and they love her very
much
Furry goes shopping for loads of hours
But doesn't buy anything apart from fancy flowers
This is my peculiar pet
A snake with fur and lots of things
This is furry the snake
The most peculiar pet
I've seen in years!

Jailah Alithia Douglas Bailey (10)
Allen Edwards Primary School, Stockwell

My Pet Kiwi

My pet is as strange as can be
At the moment it looks pretty scary
It can give you quite a fright
Especially at night
But it's not always like that you see
My pet is called Kiwi
Depending on its mood or temperature it can change
Sometimes it can have horns like a goat
Much smaller than a boat
Eyes like a fly
Not going to lie
It can also speak just like me
Out of its hands comes out frost and snow
Kind of like Elsa from Frozen, do you know that show or is it a movie I really don't know?
This is my pet Kiwi
And I'm proud to be me
This is my peculiar pet everybody.

Maryanne Grudeva (10)
Allen Edwards Primary School, Stockwell

My Lovely Peculiar Pet

Snowball doesn't like wearing pants
But she loves to dance
When she doesn't get what she wants
She's very sassy when people give her attention
she's very classy
Running around energetic
Falling down, no way, pathetic
She's very smart, as fast as a dart
She flies and she glides through the sky
She shape-shifts and has all the power in the world
She is like a ballerina when she twirls
She is a tiger and doesn't like to cry
Vicious but kind
She doesn't like to lie but looks good in a tie
This is my peculiar pet Snowball
My friend till the very end.

Soley Catherine Sanchez Gutierrez (10)
Allen Edwards Primary School, Stockwell

Bella, My Peculiar Pet

My pet panda is the most adorable thing,
She can dance, make me laugh and even sing.
What a peculiar pet!

Now she is five and her name is Bella,
We go on adventures and do everything together.
She doesn't really mind if there is stormy weather.
What a peculiar pet!

This marvellous, cute and clever pet,
Is the best present you could ever get!
Even though she frequently goes to the vet.
What a peculiar pet!

Bella's eyes are green,
The strangest ones you have ever seen.
This is my peculiar pet!

Leticia Pinto (10)
Allen Edwards Primary School, Stockwell

My Pets

My pet cheetah
Is longer than a metre

Very good at running
Also good at being cunning

The spots on his back
Look as good as a KitKat

He is very yellow
He likes to eat jello

He is very fit
He doesn't need a weight-training kit

My pet tiger
Is a very good writer

He is a very good fighter
Also a biter

He has very nice lines
Better than the number nine

He is very smart
He can also drive a kart

His tail is very pretty
He is as big as a kitty.

Nawaf Yassin (11)

Allen Edwards Primary School, Stockwell

Coco The Super-Intelligent Gerbil

Coco is a strange pet
She gives me stories to tell
Honestly, with all the silly things she has done
She belongs in a cell

She likes many things
But showers she does despise
To leave her in the bath
You need an extra pair of eyes

Although she can get lazy
Activities she loves
The ones she likes are crazy
She adores chasing doves

Even if she makes me mad
To have her, I'm glad
I will always have love
For Coco, my strange pet.

Adea Ajeti (11)
Allen Edwards Primary School, Stockwell

A Wild Life

A wild life,
One frightful night,
Some mysterious animals,
Waiting to be found,
Here comes the untamed fox,
Who went into a house and caught some socks,
Oh well, who lives in the house?
Oh well, it's a ghost who has been found,
He's the owner of the house,
The host of the show,
Comes across the bats passing the moon,
Here come rats for some food soon,
Here are mysterious creatures,
On this frightening night,
This is the wild life!

Maya Dinesh (11)
Allen Edwards Primary School, Stockwell

Evil Grog

My pet is as classic as can be
With the body of a bear and the horn of a goat
This pet is... mischievous!
With two different faces and also evil
But then this peculiar pet calls for help and is
incredibly dangerous
So you see, approach with caution
When it's noon, it's a new stage
When you see him, he will burst into rage
The hair on his head is as sharp as shards
His exotic powers shine with the stars
But he still has a long way to go.

Ejaife Dominic Adjarho (9)
Allen Edwards Primary School, Stockwell

Melanie The Baking Megalodon

She makes
She bakes
All day long

Her teeth are as sharp as a knife
Nobody knows where she sneaks at night

A few days later she goes missing
The whole town is looking

Then I see a giant rabbit hole
Then I see a mole

I go closer to it
I find myself falling into it.

I find Mrs Megalodan and everyone else who went missing while baking cakes
She is baking chocolate muffins and even cupcakes!

Asra Swadi (11)
Allen Edwards Primary School, Stockwell

Sniggle The Magical Dog

Sniggle is magical and here's why he's fierce like a tiger
Small as a mouse and when anyone gets in his way he will knock them out
He might be innocent and small in the daytime but he's a mighty, magical warrior in the night-time
He is powerful and brave
No one can get in his way
His wings are the powers that hold him up
Looking out for everyone
No one is in danger anymore
Sniggle can do anything
Sniggle is magical.

Bruna Caldeira (10)

Allen Edwards Primary School, Stockwell

Spice The Tap-Dancing Skunk

Spice is my pet
The very best, I bet

With fiery farts
Like toxic poison darts

A black and white furball
Only two feet tall

She loves to tap and dance
Hates taking naps

A dancer that's fearless
And always restless

She can be a bit of trouble
Maybe double

She is a daredevil
Definitely not peaceful

But Spice is my pet
The very best, I bet.

Aisha Kouyate (11)
Allen Edwards Primary School, Stockwell

George My Peculiar Pet

George my peculiar pet
Even smarter than its own vet
He is also very sassy
But too classy
What a peculiar pet

He is colourful and astonishing
Blink and he is gone as fast as lightning
He is incredible
But not gentle
What a peculiar pet.

He is very lazy
Also super crazy
He will never let you do your work
Always loud
He is very crazy
Very wild
What a peculiar pet!

Sariya Nevaeh Fakoya (10)
Allen Edwards Primary School, Stockwell

My Pet Gbaird

My pet is amazing
My pet is perfect
My pet likes toys
My pet likes playing with toys
Her name stands for...

G ood behaviour
B ad attitude
A mazing work
I nternet lover
R ight amount of sassiness
D rawing perfectionist

I and Gbaird are besties
We always have each other's backs
She has the right level of confidence
I love Gbaird.

Hayaat Abbas (10)
Allen Edwards Primary School, Stockwell

21

My Pet Heather

My pet is as clever as my granny Leather,
Her name is Heather,
And she loves the weather.
She isn't crazy or lazy,
But she adores daisies.
She is quite tiny,
Although she is very shiny,
And slimy.
In the night,
There is light because she shines bright.
She is fierce,
However has no ears,
Even though she has the ability to hear.
Until the end,
I will be her best friend.

Sophia Hutchinson (10)
Allen Edwards Primary School, Stockwell

Spidercat

S he has three legs and is half cat, half spider
P owers she has are fabulous
I ncredible Spidercat, she scares animals away
D angerous she can sometimes be
E xtraordinary smart she can be
R olling around on the carpet floor
C lawing at the door I closed
A gile as she runs through the house
T errifying as she bares her teeth! What a peculiar pet!

Raekwon Williams (10)

Allen Edwards Primary School, Stockwell

Who's The Gorilla Genji?

The gorilla who has the most power and is as
towering as a tower
When he is in a fight with his trusty blade
On the way he will give you shade
He can try even though he is like a normal guy
He won't stop until he gets to the top
He might look scary but he is a big teddy
He is immortal and he can make portals
He's as fast as lightning
My peculiar pet is Genji.

Jayden Andres Montoya Rodriguez (9)
Allen Edwards Primary School, Stockwell

The Stretchy-Tongued Cat

There once was a cat
Who lived in peace
He had a little secret
That his tongue was stretchable
Like a frog
Though one day
When the clouds were dark
Everything seemed to be falling apart
His evil nemesis
Had disturbed his peace
Now the cat was mad
He used his tongue to trap his enemy
Then he saved the day
By sending his enemy to space!

Daniel Galarraga (11)
Allen Edwards Primary School, Stockwell

Best Pet

My cat is the best but she needs a vest
She needs a rest,
Her name is Lily and she is very smart and silly,
She is like golden flowers and has awesome powers,
I love her to bits and I will give her lots of crisps and dips,

L ily is bright but not as bright as light,
I love her to bits,
L ove lasts long,
Y ou are the Best Pet.

Addison Ribeiro Martin (10)
Allen Edwards Primary School, Stockwell

Butterafe

B oom!

U tterly fluttery

T otally not peculiar

T errifically talented, has many talents

E ven more talented than humans!

R arely found, not very known

A ttracted easily but somehow will never be caught

F lies to what they think is danger

E xtremely rare, hope there are more species...

Efrata Weldegebriel (10)
Allen Edwards Primary School, Stockwell

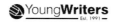

Don't Mess With The Gamer Duck

Don't mess with the gamer duck
He's half farmer
Big time gamer

Loves playing Minecraft
Three billion subscribers

He's not daft
He's very lovable
Very unstoppable

Even though he is a gamer duck
I still love him very much
Even though he loves his fans
He loves me more and is in my hands.

Fillipe Santos (11)
Allen Edwards Primary School, Stockwell

My Tiny Foxy Fly!

F lying through the air as fast as a racing car

O n a crashing car, he can fly up, up, up!

X -rays are tiny for him, especially because he is tiny

Y ou can barely see him

F lying through my house without me noticing

L ying in his tiny bed fast asleep

Y ou see my pet is peculiar.

Emily Salvador De Freitas (9)

Allen Edwards Primary School, Stockwell

My Hero Bunny

My dear devil bunny
He is a hero
Saves lives all night
He is never zero

He is fearless
Has lots of idols
Little tough man
Vile to rivals

He loves acrobatics
He is systematic
Jumps from buildings
He is fantastic

My dear devil bunny
He is always up to something funny.

Dawid Wolanin (11)
Allen Edwards Primary School, Stockwell

My Amazing Flashy Pet!

My pet is amazing
Her name is Flashy
She loves to sing
La de da!

My pet is amazing
I'm teaching her to cook
But she is not listening
So I am teaching her via a book

My pet is amazing
Truly magnificent
She wants to be just like me
But she's fine because she is different!

Teoni Ranku (10)
Allen Edwards Primary School, Stockwell

Power Dog

P owerful, particular, peculiar
O verpowering he broke the door
W inner, wonder of the world
E xcited, extraordinary
R espectfully he ran to his super house

D angerously he used his laser
O verpowered he lasered the robber
G igantic he jumped high.

Sion Gonzales (7)
Allen Edwards Primary School, Stockwell

The Rich Unihamster

I'm a hamster
Acting like a full-on gangster

They all love me
Because of all the money

I eat like a pig
'Cause it's my thing

Don't make me sad
'Cause you know what's coming your way

Just come to me
And I will help you find your way.

Oluwafunmilayo Ilori (11)
Allen Edwards Primary School, Stockwell

Blobster

B lobster is a friendly one
L ight and cautious, not much fun
O verall a caring ball
B etraying only those in fraud
S taying in London, not abroad
T his blob is one of a kind
E xciting to find
R eady to approve with some new moves.

Maia John (11)
Allen Edwards Primary School, Stockwell

Crimson

C razy Crimson goes to the park
R idiculous Crimson gets his mark
I n his test, he flew past
M agnificent Crimson missed the bus
S illy Crimson makes a mess
O f course Crimson tries his best
N othing can stop Crimson, yes!

Kevin Barrigah (10)
Allen Edwards Primary School, Stockwell

Quiver Snake

My slithering snake
Never likes to wake
He is a fast wizard
Would eat a lizard

He has venom teeth
It burns like heat
He is never beat
But he is not neat

You can't hold him like a teddy
He is very deadly
And he is heavy.

Jameel Opeloyeru (10)
Allen Edwards Primary School, Stockwell

Tedd The Shape-Shifter

In May
The start of the day
It was hot
I saw a shark
It ate fish bait
It had teeth made for beef
When it shape-shifts
It takes lift
As soon as we met
I made it my pet
It was not fun
But I got it done
However, I wanted to run!

T-jhon Simms-Wright (10)
Allen Edwards Primary School, Stockwell

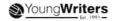

Max The Mighty Meerkat

M eat lover
E ats liquorice
E ars very huge
R oller skating
K ing of skating
A thletic
T ree climber

M ax my mighty
A ll-time favourite
e **X** tra love for me all the time.

Ana Assunção Cardoso Kaziuk (11)
Allen Edwards Primary School, Stockwell

Fancy Frog

I'm a fancy frog
I sit on a log
It's basically my throne
I don't use a phone
I really like to hop
To the bop
I like to jump
And make a big thump
Time to say goodbye
So I can eat a fly
So see ya later
Alligator!

Rosie Button (11)
Allen Edwards Primary School, Stockwell

Mika The Artistic Hare

I am Mika the artistic hare
With a pair of black ears
When I show off my art
Bart would make fun of it
Even if I feel sad
I don't think my art is bad
So next time someone says your art is worse than dry hair
Just turn away like a hare!

Abigail Oteh-Nowak (10)
Allen Edwards Primary School, Stockwell

Wolfie The Dancing Wolf

W iggle like a snake
O h you look like the wonderful bright sun
L ook so lazy, you walk like a lazy bee
F erociously snarls and growls
I ncredibly like a famous cucumber
E xpensive like a rich dog.

Mara Sequeira (10)
Allen Edwards Primary School, Stockwell

The Magnificent Misty

M isty, that's my pet's name
I ncredible, she flies with wings of flames
S wift. She's like a superspy
T remendous. You'll see her in the night sky
Y es. She's a very peculiar pet.

Yassmin Araho (9)
Allen Edwards Primary School, Stockwell

Under The Sea

Under the sea
Where all the
Fish will be
Having so much fun
Not worrying
About the sun
All the fish run
From the prawn
That has a gigantic gun
All the fish sung
While the whale told a pun.

Emily Salvador de Freitas (11)
Allen Edwards Primary School, Stockwell

My Dog

Likes to walk to the park
My dog likes to swim
She likes her friends
She likes eating food
She likes playing on the iPod
She likes to climb the tree
She likes to fly to the moon
She is light like a star.

Stella Lau (9)
Allen Edwards Primary School, Stockwell

My Crazy Cat

My crazy cat
He likes to eat rats

He sometimes does raps
While wearing a top hat

He likes to take long naps
And run many laps

He's not really fat
But good at combat.

Rakan Yassin (11)
Allen Edwards Primary School, Stockwell

Sirius Footballer

S irius, like a footballer
I ncredible like a backflip king
R un like Usain Bolt
I 'm as cool as a famous person
U nbeaten king
S pecial king.

Jahvay Ottway-Hay (10)
Allen Edwards Primary School, Stockwell

Jambo

J ust a cat
A tabby cat named Jambo
M aybe a little too strange
B ut really quite cute and all that
O h and he's very smart and fun to ride too!

Carolina Ramos (10)

Allen Edwards Primary School, Stockwell

Nooree The Mouse

M y magical Nooree
O nly helps people
U ses magic for good only
S ings lots of lines per day
E xtraordinary.

Isabelly Bernandes (10)
Allen Edwards Primary School, Stockwell

Unidog

U nique artist
N ice
I ncredible friend
D angerously messy
O rdinary pet
G reat singer.

Shaila Villavicenco (10)

Allen Edwards Primary School, Stockwell

Crazy, Nice Dog

There once was a dog called Roni
He had some nice honey
He sat on a bunny
While he was using money
Then brought home a block and a rock
He stopped and looked around
And then he found a pound
Then he had a runaround
He took a look
In a book
And then he said, "Woof, woof!"
I took him on a walk
And we had a talk
I talked to the dog
Then he met a hog
He had a little sob
But he did not rob
He heard a knock
And he suddenly got hot
He then heard a pop
He went to check

There was nothing there so next
He went to the park
And heard a bark
He went out at dark
He saw a sight
Soon it was light.

Neve Mulligan (8)
Caen Community Primary School, Braunton

Teddy The Cat-Dog

T eddy is my one-of-a-kind cat,
E ven though she mostly acts like a dog.
D addy finds her really funny,
D o you know she sits, lays and eats like a dog.
Y ou might think she is a dog, but she is a cat. My Teddy.

C an you see now that she is a cat-dog?
A dventurous, she climbs like a leopard,
T errifyingly, she hunts like a wolf.
-
D ownpour, not wet, she hides under cars,
O n hot days, she rolls in the sun, or lays on my bed.
G argantuan cats are barking like mad.

Dilly Littlewood (8)
Caen Community Primary School, Braunton

Gerty

Gerty is an extraordinary giraffe,
She certainly is game for a laugh,
A special trick she does possess,
I wonder if you can guess...
Do you have a ball or three?
Gather round with your family,
Are you ready for the show?
Go Gerty, go, go, go!
She tosses the ball up into the air,
The excitement is almost too much to bear,
Gerty juggles the balls so well,
Making sure not one of them fell,
Gerty is my incredible friend,
I hope her antics never end.

Martha Griffiths (8)

Caen Community Primary School, Braunton

My Dizzy Dog

I have a playful dizzy dog called Lily, with her hair
as black as coal
She goes all dizzy when we are delighted and gets
really excited
Even though she can whirl like a girl, when she is
getting her food Lily likes to be a dude
If she sees a weed and needs to put it on a lead
She goes all dizzy and whizzy
When she is lying down, guess what?
She turns into a clown
She spins around and around until we frown
My dizzy dog is the best peculiar pet

Matilda Powell (8)
Caen Community Primary School, Braunton

Tiny

I have an elephant called Tiny, he is a little bit whiny.
He is an elephant.
He likes to eat but doesn't like meat.
He is an elephant.
He likes books and cares a lot about his looks.
He is an elephant.
He loves mudbaths and big jolly laughs.
He is an elephant.
He travels in a herd and loves lemon curd.
He is an elephant.
He throws me high into the air, we look such a funny pair.
He is my elephant.

Thomas Griffiths-Jones (8)
Caen Community Primary School, Braunton

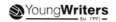

A Squirrel That Was Scared To Climb

S yril the red squirrel was

Q uite scared to climb high

U ntil one day a dog bounded by

I n pursuit of his bushy tail

"R un little Syril!" his mum said with a wail

"R emember you must try!"

E ager to escape he began to climb high

L ooking down at the dog and feeling so proud

"S afe and sound!" he shouted out loud.

Kush Bailey (8)

Caen Community Primary School, Braunton

Tortoise Michelle And Her Wheels

Michelle likes to cruise as fast as she can,
Down the windy road where she meets a curious man.
The man asks "Why do you have wheels?"
Michelle replies "It's faster than heels!"
But all of a sudden Michelle comes to a stop,
Because one of her wheels did a noisy big pop.
"Oh well" says Michelle, "I can just go home"
So she pulls in her head and is home alone.

Effie Dean (8)
Caen Community Primary School, Braunton

Terry The Turbo Tortoise

Terry the turbo tortoise eats his rocket lettuce
lunch
He can feel his energy building with every munch
and crunch
Terry the turbo tortoise needs to go for a run
He loves to have a sprint and thinks it's really fun
Terry the turbo tortoise's friends think it is really
cool
They all cheer him on since he is the fastest in the
school!

Noah Scott (8)

Caen Community Primary School, Braunton

Rock 'N' Roll Rat

Robbie the rock 'n' roll rat,
He's better than a dog or cat.
He plays the bass
At a tremendous pace
Can you imagine that?

He's such an incredible pet
And he rarely needs the vet.
If I'm feeling sad
He'll play something rad
Which helps me forget I'm upset.

Maisie Delaney (8)
Caen Community Primary School, Braunton

Ted The Wonder Dog

I love my dog who is called Ted,
He has a collar that is rosy red,
He really is small and cute,
If only he could play the flute,
He could be in a rocking band,
As long as he could understand,
When to woof and when to bark,
So we could perform at the park!

Freya Poulter (7)
Caen Community Primary School, Braunton

My Funny Cat

My cat doesn't eat mice
Because they are not nice
My cat likes sunbathing in the rain
My cat likes sleeping on the train
My cat sat on the mat.

Lucas Smart (8)
Caen Community Primary School, Braunton

My Pet Snagon (A Paradelle)

My beloved Snagon is part snake and a dragon,
My beloved Snagon is part snake and a dragon,
My Snagon is adorable, playful and clever,
My Snagon is adorable, playful and clever,
People always run away screaming,
They look at him like he is a mutated rat.

Me and Snagon were doing our daily walk to the park,
Me and Snagon were doing our daily walk to the park,
There were 'No Snagon' signs all over the park,
There were 'No Snagon' signs all over the park,
We were disappointed because we couldn't go to the park,
Life is unfair.

There was a cat scratching people that was allowed in,
There was a cat scratching people that was allowed in,

Pandog, Snagon's friend, was in the park getting stared at,
Pandog, Snagon's friend, was in the park getting stared at,
There was a dog pooing on the grass, the owner not picking it up,
I could try to disguise Snagon but it would not work.

This is unfair, people run away screaming,
Upset, disappointed, we can't go to the park,
They look at him like a mutated rat,
There is a 'No Snagon' sign in the park,
A dog pooing on grass, owner ignoring it,
If I could try to disguise Snagon it wouldn't work.

Alfie Cochrane (10)
Dormanstown Primary School, Redcar

My Pet Shilon (A Paradelle)

My beloved Shilon is part shark, part lion, he is so loving,
My beloved Shilon is part shark, part lion, he is so loving,
My beloved Shilon looks scary but really he is like a big teddy bear,
My beloved Shilon looks scary but really he is like a big teddy bear,
He can be chaos.
He is the one for me, I will never leave him.

He felt very sad because he wasn't allowed at his favourite Easter egg hunt,
He felt very sad because he wasn't allowed at his favourite Easter egg hunt,
Never judge an animal by how it looks, especially Shilon,
Never judge an animal by how it looks, especially Shilon,

My Shilon was so sad by how he couldn't be
bothered to play.
The strict owners were so mean.

The rabbit who's popping cream eggs for kids,
The rabbit who's popping cream eggs for kids,
And that dog who's dealing candy and bullying
kids,
And that dog who's dealing candy and bullying
kids,
Why is it not Shilon? Life is chaotic!

Shilon's life is chaotic,
There are so many strict people, they are so mean,
He couldn't be bothered to play, he was so sad,
All that candy getting eaten by that dog,
This is chaos,
Park managers.

Leo Slater (10)
Dormanstown Primary School, Redcar

Sneaky And Unpredictable

Intelligent and smart
Intelligent and heavy
Heavy is wide
Heavy is unique
Unique is phenomenal
Unique is remarkable
Remarkable is fantastic
Remarkable is passionate
Passionate is determined
Passionate and wise
Wise is strong
Wise and brave
Brave is mighty
Brave is courageous
Courageous is exciting
Courageous is extraordinary
Courageous and respectful
Respectable and trustworthy
Respectable and playful

Playful is adorable
Playful and friendly
Friendly is polite
Friendly and curious
Curious is thrilling
Curious and awkward
Awkward is entertaining
Awkward is foolish
Foolish is funny
Foolish and agile
Agile is sly
Agile and sneaky
Sneaky and unpredictable
Sneaky and miniature
Miniature is small
Miniature and loyal
Loyal is kind
Loyal and caring
Caring is being together
Caring and vulnerable
Venerable is weak
Vulnerable is stubborn

Stubborn is naughty
Stubborn is slow
Slow and patient
Slow and noisy
Noisy is loud
Noisy and distracting
Distracting is normal
Distracting and suspicious
Suspicious...
Normal...

Spencer Mitchell (10)

Dormanstown Primary School, Redcar

Mischievous Monkeys

Wild is their character
Wild in the forest
Forest is their home
Forest is where they play
Play and spin
Play and run
Run away from the hunters
Run fast from where they lay
Lay in the trees
Lay gorgeously
Gorgeously they are
Gorgeously they do tricks
Tricks are why they are cool
Tricks are why they are funny
Funny as can be
Funny and cool
Cool and mischievous
Cool and vicious
Vicious...
Mischievous...

Max Tighe (10)
Dormanstown Primary School, Redcar

A Friendly Penguin

Smooth is a penguin
Smooth and clever
Clever is a penguin
Clever and protective
Protective as a penguin
Protective and vicious
Vicious is this penguin
Vicious and playful
Playful is the penguin
Playful and outgoing
Outgoing is the penguin
Outgoing and soft
Soft is a penguin
Soft and unique
Unique is this animal
Unique and heavy
Heavy is this creature
Heavy and plump
Plump is this penguin
Plump and giant

Quaint is this penguin
Quaint and collaborative
Collaborative and sweet
Sweet is this animal
Sweet and healthy
Healthy is this penguin
Healthy and active
Active is this penguin
Active and caring
Caring is this creature
Caring and friendly
Friendly is this beast
Friendly and stiff
Stiff is this animal
Stiff and strange
Strange is this creature
Strange and cheerful
Cheerful is a penguin
Cheerful and fluffy
Fluffy is this penguin
Fluffy and ecstatic

Ecstatic is this animal
Ecstatic and fierce
Fierce is the penguin
Fierce and compassionate
Compassionate and affectionate
Affectionate and cute
Cute...
Affectionate...

Lucie-Rose Stubbs (9)
Dormanstown Primary School, Redcar

Dumbo

Tanka poetry

This is my cute pet
When she's mad she flaps her wings
Dumbo is her name
To work I always take her
And she keeps me company

She loves to party
And play with the children too
Dumbo likes the fun
And always plays with Patches
She's Dumbo's best friend for life

Dumbo is spotty
And she wears a tie-dye hat
She's tall and eats rocks
She has golden, furry wings
I cherish her to pieces.

Evelynn Trewhitt (9)

Dormanstown Primary School, Redcar

My Pet Rark (A Paradelle)

My adorable Rark, half shark, half rabbit,
My adorable Rark, half shark, half rabbit,
People think she is weird, dangerous but to me she
is lovely,
People think she is weird, dangerous but to me she
is lovely,
She loves going out, to go to the beach, she is the
cutest,
My Rark will never bite, unless someone's been
mean to me.

Never disrespect peculiar pets,
Never disrespect peculiar pets,
Poor Rark can't go to the local town,
Poor Rark can't go to the local town,
It isn't fair that peculiar pets aren't accepted,
they're rare pets!
To be honest, it's not fair.

The other pets aren't even behaving well at all,
The other pets aren't even behaving well at all,
How is that dog who is making old people fall
allowed in? Why isn't my Rark allowed?

How is that dog who is making old people fall
allowed in? Why isn't my Rark allowed?
All these pets doing horrible stuff in this town,
This is just crazy!

All this horrible stuff in this town,
It's that peculiar pet to be honest.
My Rark is the cutest,
This town is crazy.
To be honest, it isn't rare.
My Rark loves going to the beach.

Heidi Singh (11)
Dormanstown Primary School, Redcar

Scorpefly (A Paradelle)

Venomous fangs, deadly claws with a scorpion tail,
Venomous fangs, deadly claws with a scorpion tail,
The night, an ambush predator,
The night, an ambush predator,
The night, a venomous scorpion tail, deadly fangs,
Ambush predator with claws.

Lightning speed, it cannot be seen,
Lightning speed, it cannot be seen,
Strong in aerial and land combat, it's an apex
carnivore,
Strong in aerial and land combat, it's an apex
carnivore,
Strong in aerial, it cannot be seen,
Lightning speed and land combat, it's an apex
carnivore.

Highly intelligent, great senses, it is my peculiar
pet,
Highly intelligent, great senses, it is my peculiar
pet,
Don't get close, it can kill you in a flash,
Don't get close, it can kill you in a flash,

Great senses, highly intelligent, it can kill you in a flash!
Don't get close, it is my peculiar pet.

Lightning speed, venomous claws, don't get close!
Deadly senses, great fangs, it's an apex predator,
The night, cannot be seen,
Strong scorpion tail, highly intelligent on land,
It is my peculiar pet, an ambush carnivore and
With aerial combat, it can kill you in a flash.

Oscar Lund (11)
Dormanstown Primary School, Redcar

My Pet Frab (A Paradelle)

My beloved cute Frab loves to play in the water.
My beloved cute Frab loves to play in the water.
My Frab is a crab and a fish, people think he's weird.
My Frab is a crab and a fish, people think he's weird.
He knows lots of tricks like spin and jump.
I'll love him forever, no matter what happens.

Never judge a sea creature by how it looks.
Never judge a sea creature by how it looks.
My poor Frab cannot play at the beach, it's unfair!
My poor Frab cannot play at the beach, it's unfair!
He's depressed because he sees cats and dogs playing.
It's not fair!

Why is my Frab not allowed but all the naughty animals are?
Why is my Frab not allowed but all the naughty animals are?
There's a jellyfish stinging kids! My Frab would never do that!

There's a jellyfish stinging kids! MyFrab would never do that!
He is very mad and he is pinching my shoe.
That beach is strange.

Cats and dogs are pinching my shoe.
Strange animals jumping like they're mad.
Playing tricks.
But no matter what happens, Frab knows I love him.
At the beach he is sad.
Sad because he sees it's not fair.

Charlie Cupples (11)
Dormanstown Primary School, Redcar

Chamnersnake (A Paradelle)

Brilliant everywhere in combat, dangerous animal,
Brilliant everywhere in combat, dangerous animal,
Fast, sneaky and sly, watch the Chamnersnake fly,
Fast, sneaky and sly, watch the Chamnersnake fly,
Dangerous Chamnersnake, fast and sly,
Watch the sneaky, brilliant, combat creature fly.

Super tall, incredibly long, watch this creature transform,
Super tall, incredibly long, watch this creature transform,
Find it in the wild, tame it if you dare,
Find it in the wild, tame it if you dare,
Watch this wild creature, tame it if you dare,
It incredibly transforms super tall and long.

Ferocious, agile and scaly, clever clawed myth,
Ferocious, agile and scaly, clever clawed myth,
Extraordinary and marvellous,
Extraordinary and marvellous,

Extraordinary myth, ferocious and agile,
Clever, marvellous, scaly, clawed.

This brilliant and extraordinary creature incredibly transforms,
Clever, scaly and marvellous,
Dangerous myth, super tall and long,
Tame it if you dare,
Watch the wild Chamnersnake, fast sneaky, sly fly
Ferocious, agile animal, find it in the wild,
Watch the combat everywhere.

Jack Molyneux (11)
Dormanstown Primary School, Redcar

Courageous Cat

Quiet and lazy
Quiet as a kitten
Kitten is cosy
Kitten is cute
Cute and playful
Cute and lovable
Lovable and soft
Lovable and warm
Warm and cuddly
Warm and fluffy
Fluffy and mischievous
Fluffy and independent
Independent and trustworthy
Independent and clever
Clever and innocent
Clever and curious
Curious and smart
Curious and sneaky
Sneaky and calm
Sneaky and clumsy

Clumsy and soothing
Clumsy and athletic
Athletic and sweet
Athletic and elegant
Elegant and gorgeous
Elegant and heart-warming
Heart-warming and furry
Heart-warming and active
Active and shy
Active and adorable
Adorable and energetic
Adorable and gentle
Gentle and friendly
Gentle and trainable
Trainable and likeable
Trainable and kid-friendly
Kid-friendly and beautiful
Kid-friendly and unique
Unique and fast
Unique and small
Small and brave
Small and relaxed

Relaxed and trusty
Relaxed and graceful
Graceful and precious
Graceful and loyal
Loyal and fuzzy
Loyal and wonderful
Wonderful...
Fuzzy...

Lucy Peirse-Pallister (9)
Dormanstown Primary School, Redcar

Peculiar Pet

Tanka poetry

Jeremy is cute
He strokes my leg when I'm down
He's unique to me
Sometimes I take him to work

He asks for long walks
And loves rolling on the grass,
People stare at him
When I realise I shout
"Please don't stare at my treasure!"

My pet has small humps
With a funny giraffe neck
A red horse torso
And small, black, lumpy legs too
That's why people stare at him.

Mollie Scott (8)
Dormanstown Primary School, Redcar

My Pet Mingo (A Paradelle)

My beloved Mingo is a flamingo and a moose,
My beloved Mingo is a flamingo and a moose,
She is wonderful, sometimes she even asks to go swimming,
She is wonderful, sometimes she even asks to go swimming,
She loves to sleep quite peaceful most of the time,
Probably the best pet to sit on the sofa and cuddle with.

Never judge an animal by how it looks,
Never judge an animal by how it looks,
These animals are allowed in the pond at the park, why isn't Mingo?
These animals are allowed in the pond at the park, why isn't Mingo?
Why doesn't anyone appreciate my Mingo?
It's not fair.

That duck that is splashing kids is allowed in, why isn't Mingo?
That duck that is splashing kids is allowed in, why isn't Mingo?
OMG, that is so naughty!
OMG, that is so naughty!
That dog is peeing in the pond, why isn't my pet Mingo allowed?
My Mingo is really upset.

That dog is probably peeing,
My Mingo is upset,
My Mingo is the best pet to sit on the sofa and cuddle with,
My pet Mingo isn't allowed,
Appreciate my loved Mingo,
Why doesn't anyone?

Echo Trewhitt (10)
Dormanstown Primary School, Redcar

Deadly Dinosaur

Wild and greedy
Wild as a dinosaur
Dinosaur is bloodthirsty
Dinosaur is horrible
Horrible and old
Horrible and scary
Scary and demonic
Scary and rapid
Rapid and dangerous
Rapid and strange
Strange and scaly
Strange and strong
Strong like an ox
Strong and loudly chewing
Loudly chewing flesh
Loudly chewing bones
Bones broken
Bones and blood
Blood from the mouth
Blood dripping down

Down they go
Down they go by a dinosaur
Dinosaur is full
Dinosaur is psychotic
Psychotic and wise
Psychotic and untamed
Wise and one of a kind
Wise and vast
Vast and fast
Vast and ferocious
Ferocious like a crocodile
Ferocious and mean
Mean and nasty
Mean and evil
Evil as a hippo
Evil as a tiger
Tiger was eaten
Tiger was mangled
Mangled and dead
Mangled by dinosaur
Dinosaur is insane
Dinosaur is crazy

Crazy and fierce
Crazy and destructive
Destructive and massive
Destructive and savage
Savage and terrifying
Savage and cruel
Cruel...
Terrifying...

Elizabeth Swinhoe (10)
Dormanstown Primary School, Redcar

My Pet
Tanka poetry

I cherish my pet
He is rather aggressive
But adorable
Always I take him to work
He's always jumping around

He's always running
His favourite game is catching
And likes other pets
But sometimes he fights them off
They always make friends again

My pet is so weird
I don't care about that though
People sit and stare
Sharker always chases me
He always stinks of salmon.

Joshua Mitcheson (9)
Dormanstown Primary School, Redcar

Slow Sloths

Small and lazy
Small and cute
Cute and aimless
Cute as a sloth
Sloths are hairy
Sloths are slow
Slow and steady
Slow moving
Moving up trees
Moving before they get mad
Mad and crazy
Mad as lazy bones
Lazy bones are sloths
Lazy bones are sluggish
Sluggish and lazy
Sluggish like snails
Snails are slimy
Snails are different colours
Colours are plants
Colours are nice
Nice are pets

Nice are people
People love sloths
People love helpers
Helpers are friendly
Helpers like missions
Missions are cool
Missions are hard
Hard are enclosures
Hard workers like teachers
Teachers like their young
Teachers and companions
Companions to other sloths
Companions to other animals
Animals are slow
Animals are fast
Fast as their prey
Fast as they should be
Be yourself
Be known in the forest
Forests are dark
Forests are quiet
Quiet as can be

Quiet and furry
Furry are they
Furry and cuddly
Cuddly and sassy
Cuddly and messy
Messy...
Sassy...

Noah Rushforth (10)
Dormanstown Primary School, Redcar

My Cute Pet

(Tanka poetry)

I love my cute pet
He's so sassy but funny
He is quite unique
Harold is great at helping
He helps me with the top shelf

When I get his lead
He always grabs it off me
It's his daily walk
To the fun play park and back
He pants and drools with delight

Harold loves to eat
Especially sea bass meat
It stinks terribly
I use up so much Fabreeze
But it still stinks awfully.

Finley Dee (9)
Dormanstown Primary School, Redcar

Chaotic Crocodile

Demonic and crazy
Demonic and angry
Angry and vicious
Angry and dangerous
Dangerous and vast
Dangerous and mysterious
Mysterious and sly
Mysterious and suspicious
Suspicious and horrible
Suspicious and scaly
Scaly and slimy
Scaly and huge
Huge and evil
Hige and chaotic
Chaotic and erratic
Chaotic and mad
Mad and fearful
Mad and terrific
Terrific and greedy
Greedy and massive
Greedy and destructive

Destructive and messy
Destructive and savage
Savage and insane
Savage and terrifying
Terrifying and large
Terrifying and independent
Independent and unique
Independent and lonely
Lonely and sneaky
Lonely and wild
Wild and curious
Wild and old
Old and wise
Old and ordinary
Ordinary and prehistoric
Ordinary and amazing
Amazing and remarkable
Amazing and ferocious
Ferocious and massive
Ravenous and psychopathic
Ravenous and despicable
Despicable and animal

Despicable and ancient
Ancient and dirty
Ancient and feisty
Feisty...
Dirty...

Lola Sill (10)
Dormanstown Primary School, Redcar

Fluffy The Drago

(Tanka poetry)

Fluffy the drago
Is rather questionable
He's always jumping
Around like a great big clown
Bouncing on a softened ground

He asks me to play
But he tries to fly away
Tiredly he falls
When he hits the rocky ground
He always has a big frown

Even though he's cute
And very adorable
His gorgeous gold wings
Are attractive and fancy
However, you might get slapped.

Charlie Briggs (9)
Dormanstown Primary School, Redcar

Playful Hamster

Healthy and furry
Healthy as a hamster
Hamster is cute
Hamster is soft
Soft and crazy
Soft and lazy
Lazy and grumpy
Lazy and annoying
Annoying and stubborn
Annoying and noisy
Noisy and mysterious
Noisy and silly
Silly is funny
Silly is goofy
Goofy and clumsy
Goofy and unique
Unique and fast
Unique and sweet
Seet and spoilt
Sweet and loyal

Loyal and kid-friendly
Loyal and trustworthy
Trustworthy and pleasant
Trustworthy and hilarious
Hilarious and intelligent
Hillarious and active
Active and well-bred
Active and precious
Precious is wonderful
Precious is joyful
Joyful and hyper
Joyful and chubby
Chubby and cuddly
Chubby and delicate
Delicate and beloved
Delicate and mischievous
Mischievous and rebellious
Mischievous and sly
Sly and daring
Sly and sensitive
Sensitive and agile
Sensitive and amazing

Amazing and beautiful
Amazing and clean
Clean and quick
Clean is fun
Fun is small
Fun is super
Super...
Small...

Leonie Mitchell (10)
Dormanstown Primary School, Redcar

Peculiar Pet

Tanka poetry

Dranile likes to fly
Around the local fun park
He's fun to be with
Sometimes we ride to the shop
I love my doggy Dranile

He is my best friend
I will never let him go
He loves me a lot
In fact I take him to work
Just so he can help me out

Swimming he enjoys
And soars over the ocean
With his wings flapping
Gracefully in the blue sea
He's my peculiar pet.

Elliott Worton (9)
Dormanstown Primary School, Redcar

Destructive Dog

Sleepy and lazy
Sleepy is a dog
Dog is playful
Dog is happy
Happy and jumpy
Happy and calm
Calm and cuddly
Calm and sneaky
Sneaky and agile
Sneaky is cute
Cute and smelly
Cute and noisy
Noisy and adorable
Noisy and fluffy
Fluffy and well-fed
Fluffy and chewing socks
Chewing socks and pens
Chewing socks and loyal
Loyal and easy to train
Loyal and wild
Wild and gentle

Wild and protective
Protective and big
Protective and dirty
Dirty and huggable
Dirty and clumsy
Clumsy and entertaining
Clumsy and greedy
Greedy and cheeky
Greedy and likeable
Likeable and wonderful
Likeable and active
Active and scruffy
Active and friendly
Friendly and sensitive
Friendly and lovable
Loveable and small
Loveable and scared
Scared and fat
Scared and fluff ball
Fluffball and shy
Fluffball and funny
Funny and little

Funny and furry
Furry and fine
Furry and small
Small and clean
Small and licks a lot
Licks a lot...
Clean...

Summer Markland (10)
Dormanstown Primary School, Redcar

My Peculiar Pet

(Tanka poetry)

This is my strange pet
She is called Sammy the snog
My pet is so cute
Sammy the snog has brown dots
My bizarre pet has black clothes

My pet is so odd
But I don't know what they mean
He likes to keep clean
When he's clean he turns bright pink
But I think she's pretty.

Reiley Clark-Wood (9)

Dormanstown Primary School, Redcar

Silly Monkey

Stupid and playful
Stupid and plump
Plump and small
Plump and friendly
Friendly and funny
Friendly and active
Active and brave
Active and shy
Shy and fast
Shy and clumsy
Clumsy and savage
Clumsy and foolish
Foolish and wild
Foolish and brainy
Brainy and hairy
Hairy and pesky
Pesky and cheeky
Cheeky and remarkable
Remarkable and dirty
Remarkable and noisy
Noisy and hungry

Hungry and nice
Hungry and old
Old and great
Old and young
Young and large
Young and idiotic
Idiotic and playful
Idiotic and weird
Weird and strong
Weird and loyal
Loyal and furry
Loyal and naughty
Loyal and delicate
Delicate and little
Delicate and mischievous
Mischievous and tiny
Mischievous and well-trained
Well-trained and talented
Talented and protective
Talented and helpful
Helpful and amazing
Helpful and characteristic

Creative and idle
Characteristic and sleepy
Sleepy and selfish
Sleepy and nervous
Nervous...
Selfish...

Archie Turner (10)
Dormanstown Primary School, Redcar

My Peculiar Pet
(Tanka poetry)

I love my strange pet
Gizmo is fun to play with
I cherish my pet
Gizmo can jump to play ball
When people stare I don't care

He's an eledog
He barks and has a grey trunk
My pet is crazy
My cuddly friend has two legs
One is short and one is long.

Sienna Jones (9)
Dormanstown Primary School, Redcar

Sharknicah (A Paradelle)

Adorable, colourful, dangerous, where's the
Sharknicah?
Adorable, colourful, dangerous, where's the
Sharknicah?
Lazy, messy, has no friends,
Lazy, messy, has no friends,
Lazy, adorable, where's the friends?
Colourful, messy, dangerous, it is the Sharknicah.

Tail as blue as the sea,
Tail as blue as the sea,
It can talk every and any language,
It can talk every and any language,
Tail blue as sea, any can talk,
And every language.

Gentle, clever, extraordinary, it can run, fly and
swim super fast,
Gentle, clever, extraordinary, it can run, fly and
swim super fast,
Disappears when it wants and is always on time,
Disappears when it wants and is always on time,

Disappears always on time, is extraordinary and
gentle,
It can run, swim, fly when it wants to be super
clever.

Adorable, fast talk every language, fly super,
Disappears on time, extraordinary gentle swim
always,
Tail blue, sea messy, dangerous, wants it clever,
Colour lazy, has no friends, can and any
Run when it can and where is the Sharknicah?

Chloe Jones (11)
Dormanstown Primary School, Redcar

My Pet Shrilla (A Paradelle)

My beloved Shrilla is part shark and gorilla,
My beloved Shrilla is part shark and gorilla,
My Shrilla is gentle, adorable and clever,
My Shrilla is gentle, adorable and clever,
She likes to play games and look cute,
I will love her for eternity.

Never judge an animal by how it looks,
Never judge an animal by how it looks,
Poor Shrilla is not allowed on the beach,
Poor Shrilla is not allowed on the beach,
My Shrilla smashed the floor like thunder,
Why won't people appreciate my Shrilla?

Why is there a lion scaring kids allowed in but my
Shrilla is not?
Why is there a lion scaring kids allowed in but my
Shrilla is not?
Why is there a rabbit pooping jelly beans allowed
in but my Shrilla is not?
Why is there a rabbit pooping jelly beans allowed
in but my Shrilla is not?

There is even her best friend on the beach,
There is even a goat eating books!

Shrilla is even in books,
Lover her friend, goat,
Eternity people don't look cute,
I love her games,
Thunder eating floor,
Appreciate Shrilla.

Leon Morris-Hall (11)
Dormanstown Primary School, Redcar

Panda's Delight

Round and fluffy
Round and cuddly
Cuddly and soft
Cuddly and cute
Cute and slow
Cute and rare
Rare and young
Rare and adventurous
Adventurous and furry
Adventurous and fierce
Fierce as a bear
Fierce and sleepy
Sleepy is peaceful
Sleepy is quiet
Quiet and camouflaged
Quiet and playful
Playful and fascinating
Playful and wild
Wild with thick fur
Wild and hungry
Hungry and bamboo eater

Hungry and happy
Happy and patched
Happy and maybe red
Red and white
Red and large
Large and overweight
Large and big
Big and small
Big and adorable
Adorable and distinctive
Adorable and cream
Cream and great
Cream and woolly
Woolly and warm
Woolly and amazing
Amazing and willing
Amazing adults
Adults can have cubs
Adults are protective
Protective for food
Protective mother
Mother gives love

Mother cuddles
Cuddles and nurtures
Cares for its need
Need for love
Needs and cares
Care...
Love...

Erin-Rose Cawley (9)
Dormanstown Primary School, Redcar

Red-Nosed Reindeer

I have a strange pet
That has big ears
We sometimes walk on Saltburn pier
She has four legs and two big blue eyes
And a bright red nose
That lights up the sky

I call her honey as she's sweet as a bee
I love my reindeer
She's so cuddly.

Tiana Floyd (9)
Dormanstown Primary School, Redcar

Mischievous Monkey

Energetic and active
Energetic and lively
Lively and ecstatic
Lively and happy
Happy and playful
Happy and excited
Excited and joyful
Excited and generous
generous and lovable
Generous and clever
Clever and mischievous
Clever and smart
Smart and silly
Smart and funny
Funny and cheerful
Funny and caring
Caring and cuddly
Caring and adorable
Adorable and cute
Adorable and athletic
Athletic and entertaining

Athletic and swinging
Swinging and wild
Swinging and hyper
Hyper and fun
Hyper and smiley
Smiley and fast
Smiley and soft
Soft and beautiful
Soft and foolish
Foolish and blissful
Foolish and crazy
Crazy and furry
Crazy and amusing
Amusing and enthusiastic
Enthusiastic and whimsical
Whimsical and hilarious
Whimsical is a monkey
Monkey is an animal
Monkey is a pet
Pets are loving
Pets are gorgeous
Gorgeous and delightful

Gorgeous and lovely
Lovely and wonderful
Wonderful...
Lovely...

Josie Kretowicz (9)
Dormanstown Primary School, Redcar

The Log
(Tanka poetry)

I cherish my pet
Because he's peculiar
He loves playing fetch
My pet hates baths and showers
This lovingly pet hates walks

He is beautiful
Because he's a doglion
This pet is lonely
I never leave him alone
As he will eat all the food.

Layla Earl (9)
Dormanstown Primary School, Redcar

Amazing Cats

Crazy and wild
Crazy and cat-like
Cat-like and sleek
Cat-like and sly
Sly and hungry
Sly and naughty
Naughty and keen
Naughty and gentle
Gentle and anxious
Gentle and sweet
Sweet and tough
Sweet and cuddy
Cuddly and rebellious
Cuddly and jolly
Jolly and frisky
Jolly and gentle
Gentle and anxious
Gentle and shy
Sly and tough
Shy and rebellious
Rebellious and protective

Rebellious and playful
Playful and good
Playful and wild
Wild and big
Wild and grumpy
Grumpy and mad
Grumpy and goofy
Goofy and keen
Goofy and furry
Furry and chewing
Furry and happy
Happily playing
Happily eating
Eating peacefully
Eating quietly
Quickly jumping
Quickly scratching
Scratching noise
Scratching and frisky
Frisky and scratching
Frisky and overprotective
Overprotective and fragile

Overprotective and tiny
Tiny and lazy
Tiny and cute
Cute and fine
Cute and marvellous
Marvellous...
Fine...

Coby Waller
Dormanstown Primary School, Redcar

My Peculiar Pet

Tanka poetry

I cherish my pet
Ellie Eamel loves playing
She's peculiar
People stare but I don't care
However, I still love her

Ellie is sassy
As tall as a bamboo tree
Her snout is so short
Sucking up food is tricky
But she does it gratefully.

Imogen Banbridge (8)

Dormanstown Primary School, Redcar

My Pet Cython (A Paradelle)

My beloved Cython is a python and cat,
My beloved Cython is a python and cat,
The scales are slimy and rough,
The scales are slimy and rough,
He is a protective pet,
He looks after his owner.

He is not allowed in the forest,
He is not allowed in the forest,
He won't bite, people are scared,
He won't bite, people are scared,
His eyes will blow up with happiness,
He likes to play with other pets.

The dog is biting people, he is not allowed to go in
the forest, why can't he?
The dog is biting people, he is not allowed to go in
the forest, why can't he?
Other pets are doing bad stuff but are allowed in,
Other pets are doing bad stuff but are allowed in,

Then trying to sneak in in a disguise,
Should we do that?

He likes pets but he is a protective pet,
He likes to play with other owners,
Other pets are trying to get in a disguise,
The owners say, "Should we do that?"
Their eyes are filled with happiness,
He doesn't get the love that he deserves.

Reece Clark-Wood (10)
Dormanstown Primary School, Redcar

Peculiar Pet

Cute and playful
Cute and nice
Nice and friendly
Nice and jolly
Jolly and silly
Jolly and hyper
Hyper and snuggly
Hyper and regal
Regal and cuddly
Regal and active
Active and sweet
Active and gently
Gentle and trusty
Gentle and trained
Trained and sweet
Trained and quick
Quick and crazy
Quick and wild
Wild and adorable
Wild and warm

Warm and playful
Warm and sleepy
Sleepy and fluffy
Sleepy and cute
Cute and keen
Cute and huggable
Huggable and precious
Huggable and clumsy
Clumsy and cheeky
Clumsy and perfect
Perfect and greedy
Perfect and clever
Clever and chilled
Clever and handsome
Handsome and spotted
Handsome and smart
Smart and outgoing
Smart and soft
Soft and funny
Soft and clever
Clever and zippy
Clever and kind-hearted

Kind-hearted and wonderful
Wonderful and keen
Keen and chilled
Keen and needy
Needy and brave
Brave...
Needy...

Alfie Rayson (9)
Dormanstown Primary School, Redcar

Harry The Hamster

Tanka poetry

Harry the hamster
He enjoys playing outside
He goes in his ball
For his daily exercise
Harry's so very cuddly

People stare at him
Harry is peculiar
Because he can fly
With no wings or anything
But I do not really care.

Adam Robinson (9)
Dormanstown Primary School, Redcar

A Perfect Pet (A Paradelle)

The extraordinary elephant: Ballent Charles,
The extraordinary elephant: Ballent Charles,
Clawed with acrylic nails, incredible and clever,
Clawed with acrylic nails, incredible and clever,
Clawed Charles with extraordinary nails,
The ballet elephant, incredible, acrylic, clever.

With a super skateboard and amazing ballet skills,
With a super skateboard and amazing ballet skills,
Twelve times tables and make-up is her thing!
Twelve times tables and make-up is her thing!
Super ballet board skills is her!
With tables twelve and make-up skills.

Adorable outfits to marvellous make-up pallets,
Adorable outfits to marvellous make-up pallets,
Cow flyfish (and its Cocomelon jet ski) is the best!
Cocomelon outfits and stylish jet the marvellous!
Adorable is the ski cow and its palette make-up.

Marvellous acrylic palette nails,
Twelve ski skateboard outfits, it's flyish,
Her thing is tables times super skills ballet,
(Clawed Charles) amazing elephant and a Cocollon
cow!

Heidi Swales (11)
Dormanstown Primary School, Redcar

My Peculiar Pet (A Paradelle)

Echolocation, awareness everywhere,
Echolocation, awareness everywhere,
50mph, puts the cheetah to shame,
50mph, puts the cheetah to shame,
50mph awareness everywhere,
Echolocation puts the cheetah to shame.

Clawing up walls, hunting everywhere,
Clawing up walls, hunting everywhere,
Extraordinary, gigantic echocranthasaurus
Extraordinary, gigantic echocranthasaurus
Extraordinary clawing, gigantic hunting,
Echocranthasaurus up walls, everywhere.

Poisonous tail, venomous projectiles.
Poisonous tail, venomous projectiles.
Balanced wings, blinding wings.
Balanced wings, blinding wings.
Blinding projectiles, venomous wings.
Poisonous, balanced tail.

Clawing up walls, awareness everywhere.
Echolocation, cheetah shame.
Extraordinary, 50mph echocranthasaurus.
Gigantic, hunting up walls everywhere.
Poisonous, venomous wings.
Blinding projectiles too.

Harvey Nawton-Tunnicliffe (10)
Dormanstown Primary School, Redcar

My Pet Cish (A Paradelle)

Me beloved, cute Cish is a cat and a fish,
Me beloved, cute Cish is a cat and a fish,
He is as colourful as a rainbow,
He is as colourful as a rainbow,
He likes to go into the water,
I will love him for life.

Never judge two animals by how it looks,
Never judge two animals by how it looks,
Poor Cish isn't allowed in the town,
Poor Cish isn't allowed in the town,
The town's owner never let Cish inside,
It's not fair!

The pets are causing chaos,
The pets are causing chaos,
The pets in the town are naughty,
The pets in the town are naughty,
The cat's pooing in the boot and the fish are
wetting the kids,
My Cish is going to sleep.

He loves to go to sleep,
The cat's pooing in the boot,
The fish are wetting the kids,
Going in the water,
I will love him for life,
My Cish.

Luca Charlton (11)
Dormanstown Primary School, Redcar

My Pet Cish (A Paradelle)

My beloved Cish is a cat and a fish,
My beloved Cish is a cat and a fish,
My scaly, hairy pet,
My scaly, hairy pet,
My adorable pet,
My slimy, joyful pet.

He's not allowed in the pond,
He's not allowed in the pond,
He's so cute, he won't hurt a fly,
He's so cute, he won't hurt a fly,
Now he is lonely with no fish to pet,
He doesn't even eat fish.

There is a dog pooing in there,
There is a dog pooing in there,
There is a jellyfish stinging people,
There is a jellyfish stinging people,
There is a wild crocodile too,
The water is turning green and they're worried
about Cish.

My Cish is adorable,
My Cish is adorable,
My cute pet,
My cute pet,
My slimy, cute cat fish
My joyful, scaly pet.

Steven Porteous (11)

Dormanstown Primary School, Redcar

Venom Cat (A Paradelle)

Hooks, fangs and tail, cunning,
Hooks, fangs and tail, cunning,
Slender, ambush predators,
Slender, ambush predators,
Slender hooks and fangs, cunning,
Tails ambush predators.

Sometimes lives in prides,
Sometimes lives in prides,
Venom's body build,
Venom's body build,
Sometimes Venom builds,
Lives in body prides.

Deadly choppers, for the final blow,
Deadly choppers, for the final blow,
Wolves, sheep and bears beware,
Wolves, sheep and bears beware,
Deadly choppers for the sheep,
Wolves and bears beware the final blow.

Venom's hooks, fangs and tails, beware,
Ambush choppers, lives for the final blow,

Cunning, slender body build sometimes deadly,
Sheep in prides and bears,
Predators and wolves.

Spencer Worton (11)
Dormanstown Primary School, Redcar

Snow Cheetah (A Paradelle)

Jet-like: faster than a cheetah,
Jet-like: faster than a cheetah,
Clever and dangerous, an ambush predator,
Clever and dangerous, an ambush predator,
A dangerous cheetah, faster than an ambush,
jet-like predator and clever.

Good at smelling and hearing,
Good at smelling and hearing,
He likes to go hunting,
He likes to go hunting,
Good at hunting,
He likes to go smelling.

Jumping as high as a kite,
Jumping as high as a kite,
Wild like a wolf,
Wild like a wolf,

Jumping like a wolf,
As wild as a high kite.

Faster than an ambush,
Dangerous and jet-like like a wolf,
Jumping wild like a cheetah,
Hearing and smelling like a predator,
Good at hunting and clever,
He likes to go as high as a kite.

Onyx Clarke (11)
Dormanstown Primary School, Redcar

Peculiar Monkey

Funny and joyful
Funny and wild
Wild and friendly
Wild and lazy
Lazy and spiled
Lazy and ticklish
Ticklish and likes eating bananas
Ticklish and talented
Talented and jumpy
Talented and swingy
Swingy is the monkey
Swingy and snacky
Snacky and gorgeous
Snacky and fast
Fast like a cheetah
Fast and furious
Furious and cuddly
Furious and sleepy
Sleepy and drowsy
Sleepy and mischievous
Mischievous and silly

Mischievous and angry
Angry and cute
Angry and irresponsible
Irresponsible and feisty
Irresponsible and fun
Young and fun
Young and playful
Playful and unique
Unique and quiet
Competitive and dazed
Dazed and scary
Scary...
Dazed...

Kayden Hoyle (10)
Dormanstown Primary School, Redcar

Peculiar Pet

Tanka poetry

Patches is so cute
I cherish her to pieces
She is so unique
People always look and stare
And I always question why

She is rather strange
But I don't care about that
She meows and barks
Patches sometimes wears my hats
I think it's really funny

Patches is so weird
She's a cat, cow and giraffe
A cow print she has
And the strange thing is she's pink
But she's my little baby

My pet has best friends
In fact she has a lot of them
Dumbo is the best

Patches always plays with her
When they do it's amazing

Patches make me laugh
Because she's really funny
Getting the pool out
Wearing my swimming cosy
Thinking she's on holiday!

Alice Kent (9)
Dormanstown Primary School, Redcar

My Peculiar Pet

A tanka

Grabbite is my pet
He's very furry and brill
He loves to play fetch
People say he's very odd
But I don't care about that.

Tulisa Willis (9)
Dormanstown Primary School, Redcar

Drag

A tanka

Drag is very cute
Because he's peculiar
Drog has tall legs and
Small body with purple eyes
He can fly into the sky.

Harvey Fryett (9)

Dormanstown Primary School, Redcar

A Special Pet Indeed

A very special pet I want
And it shall be named Amucasua.
I wish upon a shooting star
From all the way to the leaves above
Some people up there hear my pleas
"Give a special pet to me!"

Then all of a sudden...
Frogs turn into cats
Horses turn into hats
Birds turn into mats
And out comes my pet!

I love it dearly
I treat it freely
And it has invisibility.
It fills me up with joy.
I'm so excited I bob up and down like a bouy.
My pet is so incredible.
Its wings are even edible.

Hodan Musa (9)
Orchard Primary School, Lambeth

The Rare Species

P ints of slime found in my room
I t's my pet again
C raving for a jar of strawberry jam
K aboom, he exploded slime on me
L abelled 'King of aggression'
E xcited to be famous

J umping up and down in the frying pan
A n apocalypse in my house
C rackling less
K ind he's not, oh now he is
S tarting good behaviour
O pposite of mean
N ow he is properly trained.

Rafsan Ramin (9)

Orchard Primary School, Lambeth

The Little Angry Potato

One day there was an angry potato crossing the
road
He was looking for a code
But there was a big load
Charley ran down the road to look for a code
He was in a happy mode
The potato called out and shouted
"Argh, there is a big by over there!"
He reached out with his hands, they were bare
But he was trying to care
He wanted to share

The potato ran as fast as a cheetah
He weighed a litre
Big bossy boy being bad.

Abdullah Malik (9)
Orchard Primary School, Lambeth

Griffin Or Squarifin

My pet is outside
Training to be fast
At last
Whoosh, zoom, ping!
Go faster already!

Now let's test his powers
Shape-shifter, colour-changer
Helps him hide in danger
He's going to be a ranger

He's getting more high
Then going to fight
Gong to get them
As if he just met them
He'll get them down
But please don't frown
Because he's your hero
See you soon.

Abdullah Yahga Umari (8)
Orchard Primary School, Lambeth

The Unknown Snake

The unknown snake is a creepy snake
Who likes to eat hairy steak
An unknown creature slithering around
You won't know but he gives you a frown
Eye contact, believe me, you're in trouble

In trouble I'll come
Screaming in trouble
Until I pop its bubble

You will be so happy you will thank me
I'll say, "Reward me with a cup of tea!"
And you will say, "No!"

Mikaeel Haruna (9)
Orchard Primary School, Lambeth

Goat Mobile

G oat Mobile is super speedy
O h how adorable he is
A lways a mischievous boy
T rains are even slower than him

M issed him in a blink of an eye
O f course quicker than a vehicle
B eats everything in a racing battle
I t's hard to see when in a car
L et it out and it will leave
E nters the world of cuteness and speed.

Bilal Ahmed (9)

Orchard Primary School, Lambeth

My Special Pet - Antelpefiy

A mazing time we had together
N ever ever will we be apart
T o think my pet is weird
E ven sometimes we hurt ourselves
L et's go and play
P fft! Leave me be!
E very day he'll be with me
F orever he will stay
I 'll always help him
Y ou and I have lots of fun.

Masud Abdi (9)
Orchard Primary School, Lambeth

Impabowl

I ntelligent like a scientist

M ore like a mathematician

P lick, plick, plick in marshland

A nd watch out for those pranks

B eautiful skies and beautiful clouds

O ver the trees and over the lands

W atch out forImpabowl, this is no joke

L urk, lurk, lurk, Impabowl is here to perch.

Mubarakat Ajetunmobi (8)

Orchard Primary School, Lambeth

Hunting Bird

This bird has the speed of many other creatures
It hunts down prey and reads its features
Its clever style makes it harder
To beat the beast and to devour

With its snake head the beast can tame
Leaving a mark and writing its name
Flying with pace at night and in the day
The bird's quick agility is not lame.

Abdullahi Hassan (9)
Orchard Primary School, Lambeth

Dangerous Dog

F licker Dog is an unordnary pet
L icking ice cream
I t is more special than you think
C lever as Albert Einstein
K ind and ferocious
E lusive as deer
R emarkable as a human

D aredevil-like
O bsessed with bones
G lamorous as a rabbit.

Ayaan Hussain (9)

Orchard Primary School, Lambeth

Lemomdoski

I wanna conquer some running
I really wanna see it coming
The head is full of smartness
But its body is full of clumsiness

Lemomdoski's head
And his tiny mouse legs
It has an awesomeness degree
And makes my teachers agree
You will never be able to see
But I always let him be free.

Adam Gacem (9)
Orchard Primary School, Lambeth

Dunkin

D unkin, Dunkin, I finally found my pet
U nusual like others but mischievous just like that
N ow he is running about in the house
K angaroos like him because of his happy smile
I love it when you jump up and down
N ow you learnt you're like a shiny troll.

Hanna Ahmed (9)
Orchard Primary School, Lambeth

Oulina The Rap Star Pet

Rap star, rap star
You are as fast as a car

Rap star, rap star
You are as special as an angel

Rap star, rap star
Some people call you a legend

Rap star, rap star
You are my best friend

Rap star, rap star
You are the world's winner!

Hafsa Haji (9)
Orchard Primary School, Lambeth

Donbry

D onny is his nickname
O ne day he will find his dad
N ever ever go to the Deck of Bay
B ro, take a day again
R unning to your home
Y our name is Donbry and you are spectacular.

Abdulsemiu Rasheed (9)
Orchard Primary School, Lambeth

Dangerous Deetog

Dangerous pet
He plays fetch
He has so many bets
He never gets caught by a net
He has jets
He doesn't need a vet
Splash three times
He gets wet
Splash three times
He gets wet.

Mohamed Hassan (8)
Orchard Primary School, Lambeth

Three Tails

Wildly-clever
Graceful-flyer
Worm-lover
Old-elder
Three-tailed
Great-rapper
Super-hero
Cleverly-sly
Rhyme-man.

Mustafa Mohamed (8)
Orchard Primary School, Lambeth

Queen Squeatcha!

Q ueen Squeatcha

U nder watch of your house and she protects her owner

E ats all kinds of meat with nuts and berries on the side

E nemies beware, Queen Squeatcha is present!

N othing can stop her

S quirrel and cheetah mixed together

Q uestion her and she attacks!

U ndercover as an adorable furry creature

E xtra bits on her ears to make her hearing 100 times better

A ctual animal, don't be afraid of her kind

T ime's up, training is over!

C atches up because she is fast

H elps you when you are in trouble

A nimal and hunter, kind and fierce, it's Queen Squeatcha!

Kali Groom (8)

St Laurence CE Junior School, Ramsgate

The Bear With The Chair

Soft fur like a soft blanket
Has shiny teeth like coins
Can be deadly and vicious
Can be very tamed
My peculiar pet is cute, clever, messy, cool
My peculiar pet likes wearing silver chains
My peculiar pet breathes fire
My peculiar pet breathes fire
My peculiar pet has powers to set stuff on fire.

Huie Thomas (8)

St Laurence CE Junior School, Ramsgate

The Out-Of-Control Cat

My Kittycorn, my cute cat
Horn as sparkly as gold
Fur as soft as wool
Slowly I stroke the cute, cuddly cat
Then she gets a bushy tail
Now opens one eye and chirps like a bird
Then waves her paws in the air, attacks a mouse
and pops.

Taylor Bradley (8)
St Laurence CE Junior School, Ramsgate

Dusto 1

D usto 1 has a mucky back
U nder the pillows he falls asleep
S andy-gold with an ear-splitting bellow
T opic is his favourite thing
O nly he can see the future

1 person can't see his feet!

Harry Alger (8)
St Laurence CE Junior School, Ramsgate

Ely Cury

She can fly like an angel
She can do magic
She is an angel, rabbit, unicorn
She always flies and sleeps
She never stops buzzing fuzzy and fast and never
stops sleeping
I never mess with her because she is fuzzy but I still
love her.

Emily Walendowska (8)
St Laurence CE Junior School, Ramsgate

The Superhero Dog

Superdog is sitting there cutely
He is waiting for some crime
Superdog can fly, he is strong like a lion
He is as big as a car
Everybody loves him, especially children
A call comes in
Out of the window he flies!

Darcie Bath (8)
St Laurence CE Junior School, Ramsgate

The Penguin

The penguin is called Poopar
He can fly with his massive wings
He is as strong as a monster truck
He has beautiful pet pigs
He always feeds chocolate to his pet pigs
I feel excellent because he is good.

Oliver Purton (8)
St Laurence CE Junior School, Ramsgate

Butter The Butterfly

Butter the butterfly is very sassy
She can do magic tricks
She is messy, gentle, cute, colourful and furry
She always gets messy and she is naughty
She is never lazy or sleepy
I think she is adorable!

Elsie Rayner (8)
St Laurence CE Junior School, Ramsgate

Beautiful, Brave Barney

He is as small as a hungry ant
His ears are fluffy like a carpet
His face is like a gigantic bear
His body is like a human body
My peculiar pet is named Barney
His feet are as big as a giant tree.

Connor Gillespie (7)
St Laurence CE Junior School, Ramsgate

The Unibunny

The unibunny is a bunny but is named an unibunny
She can talk like a human
She sounds like a human
She is beautiful
She always feeds her piglets in the morning
I love my pet so, so, so much!

Mily Packman (8)
St Laurence CE Junior School, Ramsgate

Super Cat

H oneyspot is a fatty patty
O nly has a shiny gold horn
N uts shaped as its spots
E ats only peanuts
Y ay, she looks like a piece of nut cake, spots are like dogs.

Ava Rich (8)
St Laurence CE Junior School, Ramsgate

Kot The Cat And Dog

He was as furry as a furball
Teeth as sharp as a vampire's teeth
Tail as huge as an oak wood plank
Long as a raptor
Kot is as cute as a beautiful puppy
His ears are as big as a poo.

Laiton Smith (8)
St Laurence CE Junior School, Ramsgate

Maruto's Acrostic

M ean and kind

A dorable but naughty

R ude but loving

U tterly joyous

T ame as a duck

O bedient and playful - half good and half bad
this pet is!

Mylo Baker (7)
St Laurence CE Junior School, Ramsgate

Iz Fact Poem

On his tiny head he has a cute, pointy horn
He is wild, adorable, messy, furry and sassy
He sleeps on gigantic grass
Iz is sometimes grumpy
Iz is colourful
He is gentle.

Isabelle Andrews (8)
St Laurence CE Junior School, Ramsgate

Doggy Back Horn

A horn as shiny as silver and gold coins
Teeth as sharp as an indominus rex's teeth
Carefully I stroke my dangerous, colourful dog
My magnificent dog called Doggy Backhorn.

Charlie Holt (8)

St Laurence CE Junior School, Ramsgate

The Sausage Poem

My sausage pet is very weird
I know, strange!
He can jump over the fence
He always waves at people
He never cries, never ever
I always want to spend time with him.

Tyler Hoare (7)
St Laurence CE Junior School, Ramsgate

Blossom

Blossom is very beautiful
She can be insecure and lonely
She is my pet
She sits on me!
She never bites me
I will love her forever and ever with my whole heart.

Sophie Harris (8)
St Laurence CE Junior School, Ramsgate

Spike

S leeping like an owl in the day
P ointy spikes on her ears
I nvisible body
K icking anything in her path
E verybody moves away.

Darcie Carnell (7)
St Laurence CE Junior School, Ramsgate

Gangster Gorer

This gorilla is giant
He can bite through walls
He is lazy and fat
He has sharp teeth
He always sleeps on his belly
I love my pet and I serve him.

Alfie Smithson (7)
St Laurence CE Junior School, Ramsgate

Ble

The ble is very dangerous
He can eat pigs
He is gigantic
He always helps me
He never has eaten a chicken
I like killing pigs with him.

Dylan Abram (8)
St Laurence CE Junior School, Ramsgate

My T-Rex

Gentle T-rex is strong
He is sneaky
He is clever
He is scaly
He is lazy and smelly
He is as funny as funny stuff.

Peter Taylor (8)
St Laurence CE Junior School, Ramsgate

Lilly

The cat is very pretty
He can stand up on two legs
He always tries his best
He never gives up
I never give up on him.

Ella Davies (8)
St Laurence CE Junior School, Ramsgate

The Duck

There once was a duck who had lots of pumps
And he'd do anything to blame anyone for his trumps.

The duck was once sitting his driving test,
His driving instructor was not impressed.
He pumped in the car, filling it with gas,
It didn't look like he was going to pass!

During the annual two-minutes silence,
Duck broke out in a random act of bum violence.
He blamed the farting on his brother,
Duck Lies, "We're becoming one after another!"

Duck was invited to visit the Queen,
But his farting left her feeling kind of green.
Duck had a serious issue with flatulence,
And this was causing a lot of accidents.

Duck finally found a bird in which to have a wedding,
But unfortunately it ended in a beheading.

Duck's trumps blew his wife halfway down the aisle,
This delayed the wedding quite a while.

Duck, one day went to outer space,
He was treated by aliens playing the bass.
Duck also wanted to say hello,
But out of his bum came a mighty blow.

Teddy Lane (11)
Teesside High School, Eaglescliffe

The Penguin's Adventure

There once was a penguin that was a stealthy spy
He jumped off a cliff because he thought he could fly
When he fell to the ground all hope seemed lost, however, he was fine
His eyes were crossed and he waddled to his friends, however, they let out a big sigh

When he spied on the queen he saw a bag of fish
So he chased it on to a marvellous dish
When he got the fish he was thrilled
But the fish was grilled and squished

In rage he confronted her
He marched over and shouted with glee
As the queen heard this
She immediately began to plead

The penguin snuck into the palace
As he saw the wonders that were ahead
However the guard found him
And they said, "Off with his head!"

There was a penguin who was a spy
He jumped off a cliff since he thought he could fly
His eyes were crossed and he waddled to his friends
He was fine but his friends let out a big sigh.

Hadi Younis (11)
Teesside High School, Eaglescliffe

Speedy Sue

I just adopted a tortoise, her name is Speedy Sue
The vet said that she's speedy and that is definitely true
She speeds all around her cage
So maybe she could win a race

She trains hard all week long
Listening to her favourite song
She runs up hills and down the other side
Through green trees and mountains too

By June I think she'll be ready
She's running strong, she's running steady
The hard moor's 10k is next week
I am going to fill the form that enters her in

It's ten minutes before the race
Speedy Sue is ready to set the pace
I gave her some lettuce, some last-minute fuel
The gun booms loud and off she goes

The finish line is in her view
I think that she can win this, what about you?

Up on the podium, gold sparkling around her neck
The world's fastest tortoise, my Speedy Sue.

Martha Shakesheff (11)
Teesside High School, Eaglescliffe

Tigger The Digger

Yesterday I decided I wanted an extension,
So I looked around for a builder,
Until a cat caught my attention,
So I asked him.

He said, "Yes of course,"
So we arranged to meet again,
But then I said, "I need somewhere to store my house!"
And he then said we could build a stable.

I found out his name was Tigger
And his dream was to be a builder
And he loved to drive a digger,
He was very happy to build my extension.

Next week I had my extension made,
Tigger's digger was parked outside my house,
But he went a bit crazy with a spade,
I was relieved when he finally finished.

Ava Jeavons (10)
Teesside High School, Eaglescliffe

The Pig Maid

Yesterday I saw a very strange pig
Who said he was a very good maid
He worked for our own royal family
Where he was handsomely paid
He stood there in uniform red, white and blue
Trotters covered with shoes of black
He turned around to show me
The colours were the same at the back
His skirt was blue, his blouse red
A sash of white in-between
The hat on his head seemed to bounce as he turned
It all seemed exceedingly clean
We were not far away from the palace
He offered to show me the way
A talking pig, a pig who's a maid
It was the most peculiar day!

Louis Main (11)
Teesside High School, Eaglescliffe

My Cat Is A Superhero

My cat Chester, the ginger tabby one,
He flies by night and by day snoozes on.
He has bionic superpowers underneath his fur,
But the biggest power comes from his supersonic
purr.

His ears are gigantic, like satellite dishes,
Eyes so bright they will seek out your wishes,
His fur spikes up when trouble is near,
His cloak will come out and Supercat is here.

Chester will cuddle when danger has passed,
He wouldn't be Supercat without his hero mask.
No one knows when Chester will appear,
He's my ginger tabby cat who has no fear.

Coco Hawkings (11)
Teesside High School, Eaglescliffe

198

President Bunny Takeover

Something was in the air tonight,
A wave of change detected,
For the people they had voted,
And a President Bunny they elected.

"This is outrageous!" the animals cried,
"Her walk is way too hoppy!
She twitches her nose far too much!
And her ears are much too floppy!"

"Free carrots for all!" she did declare,
"And no cost for fixing your hutches.
I'm going to keep you bunnies safe...
And away from enemy clutches!"

Maisie Crowther (11)
Teesside High School, Eaglescliffe

The Salesman Fish

My friend's new fish is a salesman
Who knocks on all the doors
Asking to sell items to people that are poor
Like selling furniture so they are not sitting on the floor

Swimming around his fish tank
Going round in circles
Doing another deal with his favourite customer Frank
His favourite tables are semi-circles

My friend's new fish is a salesman
Who knocks on all the doors
Asking to sell items to people that are poor.

Ellie Charlton (10)
Teesside High School, Eaglescliffe

Rocket-Propelled Turtle

Five years ago I bought a turtle,
The fastest turtle of all time,
He had rocket boosters and laser eyes,
He wouldn't listen to anyone but spies.

One day this turtle went missing,
Leaving the whole family to start grieving,
Little did we know this turtle was fine,
Way up in the sky his shell was beginning to shine.

The wind started to pick up and the sun was going down,
So with the last of his fuel he began to head back down.

Monty Shepherd (11)

Teesside High School, Eaglescliffe

YOUNG wRITERS INFORMATION

We hope you have enjoyed reading this book – and that you will continue to in the coming years.

If you're a young writer who enjoys reading and creative writing, or the parent of an enthusiastic poet or story writer, visit our website **www.youngwriters.co.uk/subscribe** to join the World of Young Writers and receive news, competitions, writing challenges, tips, articles and giveaways! There is lots to keep budding writers motivated to write!

If you would like to order further copies of this book, or any of our other titles, then please give us a call or order via your online account.

Young Writers
Remus House
Coltsfoot Drive
Peterborough
PE2 9BF
(01733) 890066
info@youngwriters.co.uk

Join in the conversation!
Tips, news, giveaways and much more!

 YoungWritersUK    YoungWritersCW    youngwriterscw